Freedom Technique

by
JOAN LAST
Book 1

Students in the early grades are often able to give only a limited
time to technical practice. It is essential, therefore, that elementary
technical exercises are short and to the point.
These examples are designed to promote ease of movement over the
keyboard. The notes are easy to learn so that the main objective can be the
technical problem. Sequences throughout remain short, enabling the
student to include a suitable series in each practice session.

J.L.

Oxford University Press

Music Department, Great Clarendon Street, Oxford OX2 6DP

All the exercises on this page can be attempted during the first week of piano playing – (some may have to be taught by rote where the beginner is young).

BALANCED HAND AND ROTARY FREEDOM

RIGHT HAND ALONE
Legato (smooth)

1a

LEFT HAND

1b

CROSSING HANDS (for free movement)
Play each note with the 3rd (middle) finger.

repeat three times   repeat three times

2

ARM WEIGHT
Cling to the keys with the fingers.
Use full flex of the wrist, without allowing it to collapse or become flabby.
Start with the elbow slightly raised. Hold the interval for seven counts, up on eight, move arm as directed★. But make sure you do not lose the sound (firm fingers always).

RIGHT HAND

3a

★ down up down up down up down { up off

3b LEFT HAND as above one octave lower

QUICK RELEASE OF KEY
TRAVELLING UP AND DOWN THE KEYBOARD

RIGHT HAND

4a

LEFT HAND

4b

The above fingering is the easiest for the beginner, but alternative fingerings may be used, and the following version attempted.

RIGHT HAND

5a

5b LEFT HAND starts by descending as in 4b and ascends from bar 8.

ROTATION EXERCISE

RIGHT HAND

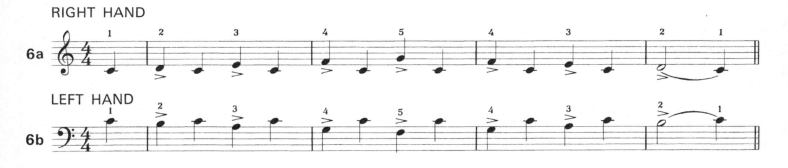

SLURS

1st beat louder. Release 2nd beat *gently*.

RIGHT HAND

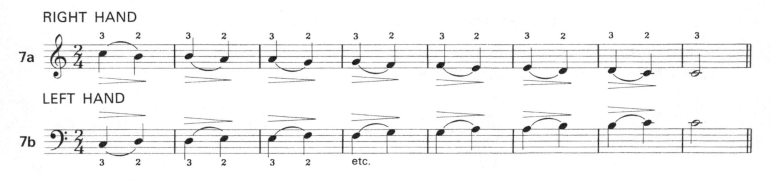

FIVE-FINGER GROUPS AND SLURS

RIGHT HAND

ARM WEIGHT (firm fingers)

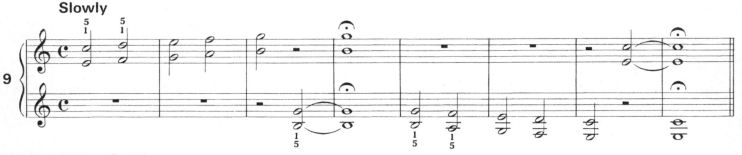

Freedom technique Book 1

STACCATO
Keep close to the keys. Use 3rd finger throughout.

When good staccato action has been achieved Ex. 10 may be played with five fingers, but do not allow fingers to fall back or wrists to become flabby (a good test—you must not see your fingernails!).

SCALE PREPARATION (free lateral movement)

RIGHT HAND uses fingers printed over the notes.
LEFT HAND uses fingers printed under the notes.

LEGATO THUMB TURN

RIGHT HAND
Repeat bars 1 to 4 several times listening for even tone.

LEFT HAND
Repeat bars 1 to 4.

SCALE SEQUENCE WITH SLURS AND STACCATO

RIGHT HAND
2nd note of each slurred pair to match the staccato that follows.

LEFT HAND

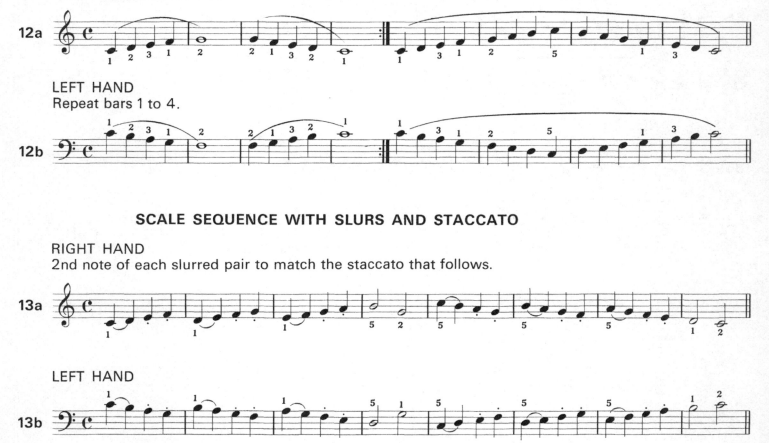

Freedom technique Book 1

ROTATION ALTERNATING WITH FIVE-FINGER GROUPS

THE CHORD (TRIAD)

QUAVER GROUPS WITH BROKEN CHORDS

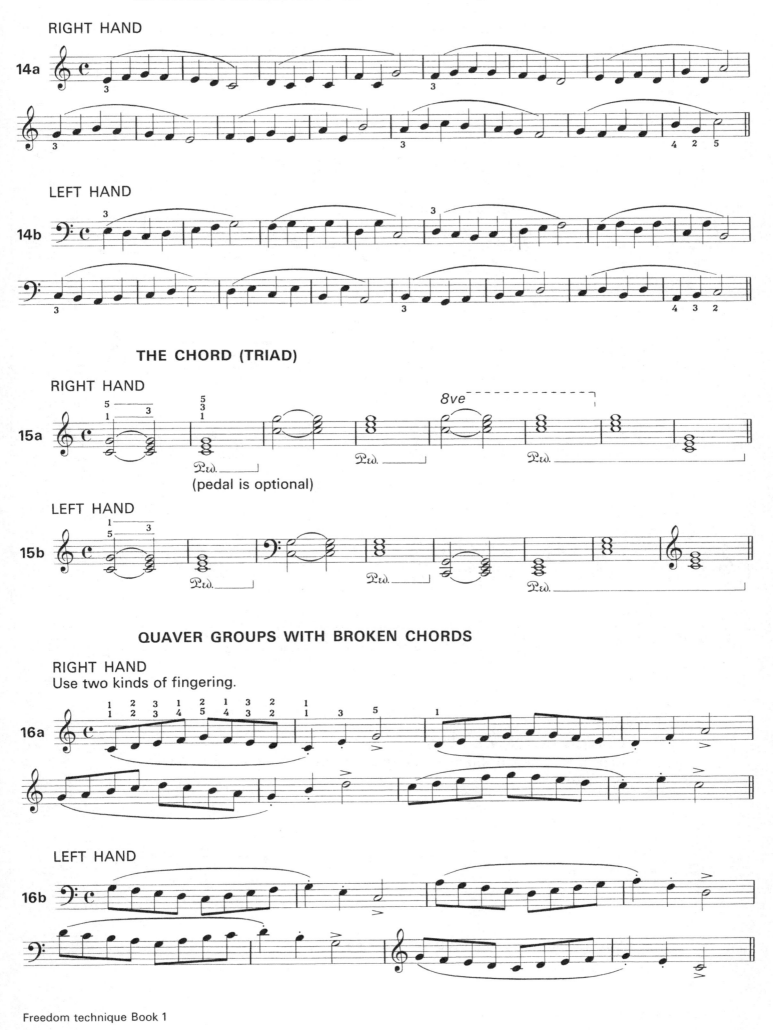

6

TONE BUILDING AND NEATNESS IN STACCATO AND SLURS

Make sure the note which comes on the 2nd beat of the bar is softer than that on the first beat.

17

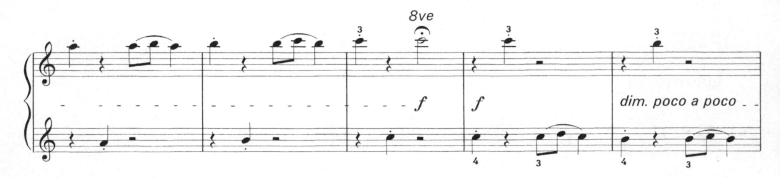

CONTINUATION OF KEYS

Repeat Ex. 12a and 12b in keys G and F, remembering that R.H. fingering in Key F will be:

18

Next repeat Ex. 15a and 15b in keys G and F.

BUILDING UP THE CHORD AND ITS INVERSIONS

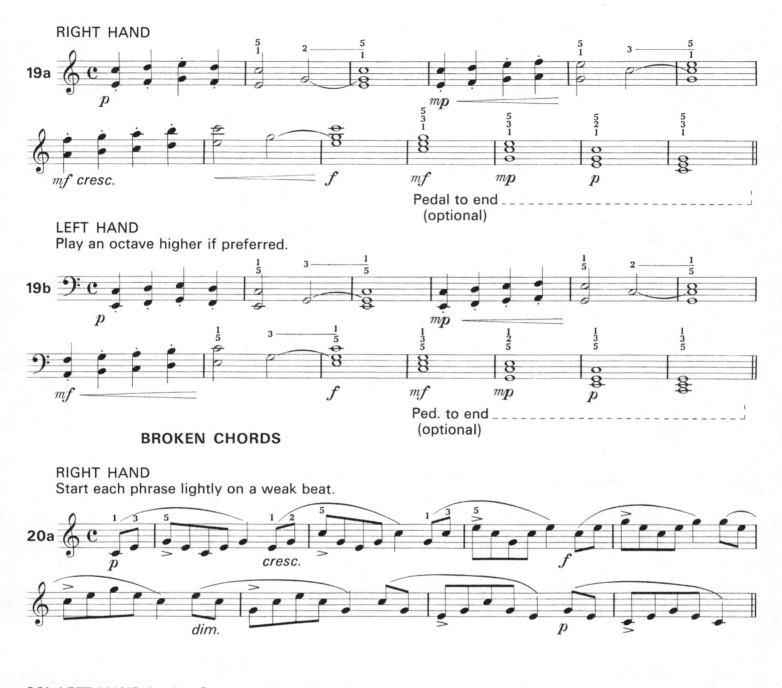

BROKEN CHORDS

RIGHT HAND
Start each phrase lightly on a weak beat.

20b LEFT HAND begins 2 octaves lower and follows right hand pattern.

SLURS—WIDE SKIPS, USING NOTES OF THE CHORD

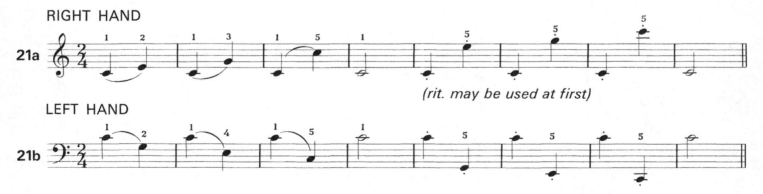

8

THE HARMONIC MINOR SCALE (A MINOR)

Now play the complete scale of A minor in each hand.

MINOR CHORDS AND INVERSIONS
Using arm weight but firm fingers

(pedal is optional)

BROKEN CHORD STUDY (MINOR KEY)

Exercises 22a to 24 inclusive are to be played in other minor keys as they are learnt.

FOR CONTROL OF THUMB AND EVENNESS IN TWO-OCTAVE SCALES
Increase the speed each week.

RIGHT HAND

LEFT HAND

TWO-OCTAVE ARPEGGIOS
Not fast. Keep accents away from the "half-way" thumb.

RIGHT HAND

LEFT HAND

SCALE AND ARPEGGIO EXERCISE
May be played in all known keys.

RIGHT HAND

LEFT HAND

Exercises 27a — 27b may be attempted with both hands in contrary motion.

TRIPLETS AND STACCATO WITH TONE BUILDING AND FADING

CHROMATIC GROUPS

RIGHT HAND

LEFT HAND

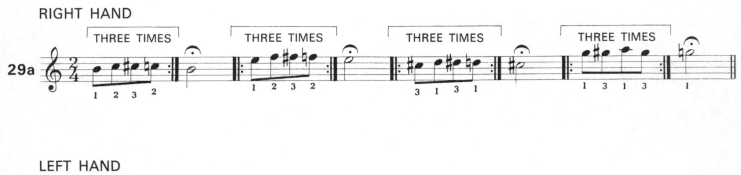

The whole of Ex. 29a may be played together with 29b in exact contrary motion (fingers co-ordinate).

CHROMATIC SCALES

RIGHT HAND

LEFT HAND

SCALE 'TUNES' FOR TRANSPOSITION
These may be played in either hand with the left hand at a suitable register.

Soften the crotchets to get the 'swing'.

IN EITHER HAND

R.H. fingering

L.H. fingering

Play exercises 31, 32, and 33 in all known keys.

MATCHING TONE BETWEEN THE HANDS

Left-hand stems down, right-hand stems up.

There should be no difference *in sound* between Ex. 34a and 34b.

SLOW PEDAL EXERCISES
Release the pedal at the moment each new harmony is heard. Press it down again when the dampers have done their work.

IN EITHER HAND

Processed and printed by
Halstan & Co. Ltd., Amersham, Bucks., England